D1252672

HIP-HOP

Hip-Hop

Nelly

James Hooper

Mason Crest Publishers

Nelly

FRONTIS Rap star Nelly has risen above a difficult childhood to become a major figure in hip-hop culture.

PRODUCED BY 21ST CENTURY PUBLISHING AND COMMUNICATIONS, INC.

EDITORIAL BY HARDING HOUSE PUBLISHING SERVICES, INC.

MASON CREST PUBLISHERS INC.
370 Reed Road
Broomall, Pennsylvania 19008
(866)MCP-BOOK (toll free)
www.masoncrest.com

Printed in Malaysia.

9 8 7 6 5 4 3 2

Library of Congress Cataloging-in-Publication Data

Hooper, James, 1957–
    Nelly / by James Hooper.
        p. cm. — (Hip-hop)
    Includes bibliographical references (p.   ) and index.
    ISBN 1-4222-0123-6
    1. Nelly (Rapper)—Juvenile literature. 2. Rap musicians—UnitedStates—
Biography—Juvenile literature. I. Title. II. Series.
ML3930.N45H66 2007
782.421649092—dc22
[B]   2006014694

Publisher's notes:

- All quotations in this book come from original sources, and contain the spelling and grammatical inconsistencies of the original text.

- The Web sites mentioned in this book were active at the time of publication. The publisher is not responsible for Web sites that have changed their addresses or discontinued operation since the date of publication. The publisher will review and update the Web site addresses each time the book is reprinted.

Contents

Hip-Hop Timeline

1974 Hip-hop pioneer Afrika Bambaataa organizes the Universal Zulu Nation.

1988 *Yo! MTV Raps* premieres on MTV.

1970s Hip-hop as a cultural movement begins in the Bronx, New York City.

1985 *Krush Groove*, a hip-hop film about Def Jam Recordings, is released featuring Run-D.M.C., Kurtis Blow, LL Cool J, and the Beastie Boys.

1970s DJ Kool Herc pioneers the use of breaks, isolations, and repeats using two turntables.

1979 The Sugarhill Gang's song "Rapper's Delight" is the first hip-hop single to go gold.

1986 Run-D.M.C. are the first rappers to appear on the cover of *Rolling Stone* magazine.

1970   1980   1988

1976 Grandmaster Flash & the Furious Five pioneer hip-hop MCing and freestyle battles.

1986 Beastie Boys' album *Licensed to Ill* is released and becomes the best-selling rap album of the 1980s.

1970s Break dancing emerges at parties and in public places in New York City.

1982 Afrika Bambaataa embarks on the first European hip-hop tour.

1970s Graffiti artist Vic pioneers tagging on subway trains in New York City.

1988 Hip-hop music annual record sales reaches $100 million.

1984 *Graffiti Rock*, the first hip-hop television program, premieres.

1993 Rapper Snoop Dogg's album *Doggystyle* is the first debut album to hit the music charts at number one.

2006 Queen Latifah becomes the first hip-hop artist to receive a star on the Hollywood Walk of Fame.

1989 DJ Jazzy Jeff & The Fresh Prince become the first hip-hop artists to win a Grammy Award.

2003 Rapper Eminem becomes the first hip-hop artist to win an Academy Award.

2005 Hip-hop artist Kanye West appears on the cover of *Time* magazine.

1989 Rap is added as a new category to the *Billboard* charts.

1997 East Coast rapper Notorious B.I.G. (aka Biggie Smalls) is murdered.

2004 First National Hip-Hop Political Convention is held in Newark, New Jersey.

1989   2000   2006

1990s Hip-hop emerges in Europe.

1996 West Coast rapper Tupac Shakur is shot and killed.

2005 Rapper Will Smith opens the Philadelphia Live 8 concert as part of 10 simultaneous concerts held worldwide to bring attention to the extreme poverty in Africa.

1989 First gangsta rap album, *Straight Outta Compton*, is released by N.W.A.

2001 The hip-hop political action group, Hip-Hop Summit Action Network, is founded by Russell Simmons.

1992 Dr. Dre's album *The Chronic* is released; it redefines West Coast rap.

2006 The Smithsonian Institute National Museum of American History announces the creation of a new hip-hop exhibition scheduled to open in three to five years.

Though Nelly dropped out of high school, he knows how important a good education is. In 2001, he returned to St. Louis to talk and play hoops with students who had good school attendance records.

1

Looking Back

In May 2001, high school students in St. Louis, Missouri, got a thrill of a lifetime. Nelly, the hip-hop superstar, paid them a visit. He even shot some hoops with students who had perfect attendance records. The next day, he DJed during an honor-student basketball game. And the following month, he was back to do it all again.

While he was in the St. Louis area, Nelly also signed autographs at a charity basketball game at Washington University. He took time to meet students personally at Sumner High School in St. Louis, and he got out on the court again with kids who had good attendance. Meanwhile, his band—the St. Lunatics—had just released their album, *Free City*. And Nelly's solo career was going strong.

Nelly was busy doing the things he enjoys most: playing sports, rapping, and encouraging kids to stay in school. He had made mistakes in his own life, and he wanted to do what he could to help other kids head in a different direction. After all, he knew what they were going through. Not that many years ago, he too had been growing up on the streets of St. Louis.

Back then, everyone had a nickname. No one would have guessed that Cornell Hayne's nickname would one day be famous.

Childhood

Cornell Haynes Jr. was born on November 2, in Austin, Texas. (Not many people know the year of his birth, however; it's a secret that Nelly doesn't share with the world.) His parents were Rhoda Mack and Cornell Haynes Sr. His father was a sergeant in the U.S. Air Force, which meant the family moved a lot during Cornell Jr.'s childhood. Until he was three, he even lived in Spain.

Eventually, though, the family settled in St. Louis, Missouri, a state with strong connections to the pre–Civil War South. In several interviews, Nelly has mentioned that Missouri is a "former slave state," and that heritage of racial **inequity** left its mark on his childhood and teenage years. Although St. Louis is a city, it has something of a small-town feel, as well as a reputation for poverty and crime. Nelly said on his Web site, "It's so small that everybody know each other. I've got a love-hate relationship with it."

During Nelly's growing up years, the city of St. Louis often stood in the place of his family. He spent most of his time on the streets, with friends his own age, as well as boys who were older than he was. His parents had divorced when he was eight years old, and Nelly was unsupervised much of the time. He told *Rolling Stone*:

> **"There was a time when my mother couldn't afford to keep me, and my father couldn't afford to keep me, so I lived with friends, with grandparents. When you're a kid, that affects you. You don't see that it's not because they don't want you. That's why you rebel."**

Nelly's rebellion got him into trouble. He was an angry little boy, and he took out his feelings of rejection and anger on other kids. The schools he attended often kicked him out for fighting. Sometimes, his mother changed his schools, hoping a fresh start would help him change his behavior (but it didn't). By the time Nelly was in middle school, he had attended more than eight different schools.

"I had a chip on my shoulder," Nelly admitted in an interview with *USA Today*. "The only way I got over that is, my mama always said she was coming back for me, and she did." Knowing he could depend on his mother to keep her word was the only security he had.

His mother was doing the best she could. She worked at fast-food restaurants and tried to make enough money to support her son. She knew the streets of St. Louis weren't a good place for a boy to grow up,

Nelly was born in Texas but spent some of the first three years of his life in Spain, where his military father was stationed. Who could have anticipated that this cute little guy would grow up to set the music world on fire?

With his parents divorced, an absentee father, and a mother who sometimes could not afford to keep him, Nelly was an angry young boy. He got into many fights and was often kicked out of school for fighting.

so finally, she packed him up and moved to University City, a quieter suburb of St. Louis.

The move was good for Nelly. He no longer got in as many fights; instead, he was involved in sports. He soon became a star player for his new school's baseball team.

In St. Louis, other kids had teased him because he was small—but now he discovered that he was built exactly right for playing shortstop. By the time he was attending University High School, college **scouts** and even some professional teams were paying attention to his talent.

Baseball helped Nelly handle the frustration and anger that had once driven him to get in fights. He told *Teen People,* "I never felt pressure, just the energy and excitement of 'Let's get it rolling.'" Succeeding at something made him feel good about himself.

Baseball also brought Nelly together with people who would help shape his future. One of these was another baseball player, named Robert Cleveland, who went by the name of Kyjuan. Kyjuan was a hip-hop fan, who noticed that Nelly had some genuine talent for rap as well as baseball.

Rap and Hip-Hop

The rapping that Nelly did as a teenager had a long **heritage**. It had grown out of the "blues," which in turn had come from African American slaves' **spirituals** and chants. In the 1940s, this music combined with jazz (another form of African American music). Rhythm and blues—or R&B—came next.

All this was happening at time when things were bad for African Americans, especially in the South, where they faced **prejudice** and **segregation**. But music gave blacks a way to rise above their circumstances.

James Brown, an African American musician, blended together blues, **gospel**, jazz, and country vocal styles to create a brand-new sound. Brown also jived and jumped as he sang. He made a new music called funk, where the beat was all-important. Funk music was meant for dancing, and its rhythm beat out loud and strong. Hip-hop and rapping were just around the corner.

A guy from Jamaica named Kool Herc started it all in New York City's South Bronx. He used two copies of the same record to turn a fifteen-second segment into a piece of music that went on and on, mixing back and forth between the two records, using the turntables as musical instruments to create a thumping new sound. And while Herc was performing with turntables, he was also **emceeing**, using his microphone to mix in jokes, boasts, and other comments. Hip-hop had been born.

Hip-hop gave black kids on city streets their very own voice. It soon became an entire culture, and rap was its music. After only a few years,

Kool Herc started the hip-hop craze in New York City. Hip-hop has grown a lot since those early days. Here, in a 2006 photo, Kool Herc is shown at a press conference announcing the Hip-Hop Exhibition at the Smithsonian National Museum of American History.

this culture had jumped from New York City across the continent to Los Angeles in California. By the time Nelly was in middle school, hip-hop had traveled all the way to St. Louis, Missouri. Rapping was cool, and it gave Nelly a chance to be good at something.

Addicted to Dollars

When Kyjuan and Nelly were fourteen years old, they put their skills to work and wrote a song together: "Addiction." Although Nelly was

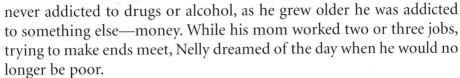

never addicted to drugs or alcohol, as he grew older he was addicted to something else—money. While his mom worked two or three jobs, trying to make ends meet, Nelly dreamed of the day when he would no longer be poor.

When Nelly was fifteen, he and Kyjuan and several of their friends formed a band, the St. Lunatics, in honor of their hometown. Besides Nelly and Kyjuan, the band included Murphy Lee (Tohri Harper), Big Lee (Ali Jones), and Nelly's half-brother, City Spud (Lavell Webb). Slo Down (Corey Edwards) joined the group a few years later.

Nelly loved rapping with his friends—but he didn't expect it to make him rich. Instead, he was counting on baseball to get him out of poverty.

While he was still in high school, the St. Louis Amateur Baseball Association **recruited** him to play. Major league teams like the Atlanta Braves and the Pittsburgh Pirates were also showing some interest in him. Nelly was sure he was on his way.

But although Nelly was a good baseball player, he wasn't good enough yet for the major leagues. Nelly didn't have the patience for the years of practice he would need before he could expect to have major-league skills. He told *Sports Illustrated*, "Baseball to me was a slow, grinding process, and I wanted the fast money, and all that. So I kind of got out of the baseball thing and went back to the **hood**."

When *Rolling Stone* interviewed Nelly, he explained his attitude a bit more: "I was down in the hood, and the money was flowing. A bat and a ball. That was taking too long."

Nelly quit high school—and he quit baseball. Instead, he turned to a fast, sure way of making money: dealing drugs.

On His Own

By the time others Nelly's age were graduating from high school, he was living on his own. In order to be sure of a steady paycheck to pay his rent, he worked part time at a fast-food restaurant. Most of his money, though, came from dealing drugs.

On the streets of St. Louis, drug dealing was a common career choice. Unemployment rates were high for African Americans; many black men didn't feel they had many choices besides drug dealing, especially if they wanted to support their families and make a decent living.

Nelly was still a teenager, but he was about to become a father. First came his daughter Chanel, and then, three years later, his son Cornell

Haynes III—Tre—joined the family. Nelly was determined to do right by his kids. He wasn't going to leave them on their own the way his father had left him when he was little.

But while drug dealing provided him with an income, he also realized that it might end up taking him away from his kids. He saw what happened to older dealers: they ended up either dead or in prison.

Baseball wasn't going to get him out of the hood, but maybe music could. Nelly listened to the greatest hip-hop artists—musicians like Rakim, LL Cool J, Run-DMC, OutKast, Goodie Mob, and Jay-Z—and he became convinced that he too could use his gift for rap to make himself a career.

But in St. Louis, hip-hop and drugs were all knotted up together. Nelly told *Rolling Stone*:

> **❝There was a point in St. Louis where dope was your currency. Whoever was bringing in the most [drugs] did the most [rap], basically. As far as reputation, the more work you had the bigger you were in rap.❞**

In other words, the more drugs Nelly dealt, the better his chances were of making it big in St. Louis's hip-hop scene. Drug deals made him connections with the top hip-hop clubs. But finally, Nelly got his chance to break free of the drug scene.

Breaking Into Music

A local production company took a liking to the St. Lunatics, and it financed their CD. The album's first single, "Gimme What Ya Got," was played over and over at St. Louis's biggest hip-hop club, Club Casino. Next, a local radio station picked up the song. The song gained fans, and the single eventually sold 7,000 copies (an amazing number for a song produced by an independent label). It was the number-one song on St. Louis's hip-hop airwaves.

But despite the song's success, the St. Lunatics still couldn't get a meeting with any major record labels. Nelly worried that the record companies had a closed mind when it came to rap coming out of St. Louis. After all, hip-hop had started on the East Coast, and eventually, it had jumped to California—but the Midwest was simply not the place to be when it came to rap.

Nelly didn't like being poor, and he dreamed of the day when lack of money would not be an issue. Then he could afford to keep himself in the fashionable style he exhibited as early as his prom in 1993.

Nelly's first adventure into music was with the St. Lunatics, named in honor of his hometown, St. Louis. When a record company only wanted him, Nelly made sure the St. Lunatics were given the chance to record as well.

Nothing had come easy for the St. Lunatics during the years they had been together. Nevertheless, they were determined to stay together. "We're all family," Nelly told *Teen People*. "We came up together from nothing."

The St. Lunatics weren't about to give up. So they created a new **demo** CD, titled "Country Grammar"; they planned on sending it around to all the big record companies. In the meantime, a DJ at St. Louis's Club Casino liked the song so much that he played it two or three times a night.

And finally, the song caught the attention of Cudda, who owned Reel Entertainment and had managed the career of Mase, a well-known hip-hop musician. Cudda got a copy of the demo—and he took it to a man he knew, Kevin Law, who had just started a new hip-hop division at Universal Records.

The St. Lunatics' big break had finally come. But it wasn't what they had expected.

Nelly's career as a solo artist took off with a bang, and it wasn't long before the music world was talking about Nelly and his music. Fans found music they could relate to, and girls found a musician they liked looking at!

Two Very Good Years

As soon as Kevin Law heard "Country Grammar," he knew he had found his new division's first artist. The executives at Universal Records didn't want all the St. Lunatics, though; they only wanted Nelly. Universal Records felt it would be less risky to use experienced professional **studio musicians** to back up Nelly (who, after all, was still an unknown).

Going Solo

Nelly wanted to be loyal to his friends—but he also wanted to take advantage of the opportunity that had finally come his way. Despite the group's determination to stay together, Nelly's friends were also loyal to him. They wanted what was best for him. So they encouraged Nelly to go out on his own. Nelly told MTV:

> **"Well, it wasn't my idea, it was a group idea. We sat down and I want to tell everybody it's not Nelly and the St. Lunatics, it's Nelly *from* the St. Lunatics, 'cause I'm still in the group, always will be in the group, started in the group and I ain't never leavin' the group. But it was something we all decided on."**

When Nelly signed the contract with Universal Records, he did what he could for the rest of his crew. The company agreed to release a CD of the St. Lunatics' music if Nelly's solo album did well. The company also promised that the St. Lunatics would be able to go on tour with Nelly.

Small-Budget Production

But Universal wasn't willing to invest much on the unknown artist. Nelly told *Rolling Stone*:

> **"We had three weeks in a little studio and a little bitty budget. When you hungry, it don't matter. We'd do two songs a day. When from where we from, you waitin' for your shot, that's all you lookin' for."**

Nelly made do with what he was offered. He felt he was speaking on behalf of everyone like him, all the black kids in the South who had come up on the streets, doing the best they could despite how few opportunities came their way. Nelly explained to *Teen People*:

> **"My whole purpose was to make people who speak Country Grammar not ashamed of how they talk, and turn it into the hot slang. *Country Grammar* is a celebration of having a national album come out of St. Louis. We're on a whole other level now, so let's kick it and in St. Louis *we kick it*!"**

Success!

Nelly may have had a small budget for his album, but the final product made waves even before it was released. Music industry magazines were buzzing with rumors about the new hip-hop artist. Once the *Country*

Country Grammar was Nelly's first album and first giant hit. His sing-along style made him different from any other rap artist of the time. In 2000, he performed at the JAM'N 94.5 Monster Jam in Boston, where this photo was taken.

Grammar video was out, MTV put it on the air, and the whole world got to see what Nelly looked like. The audience liked his looks, his voice, his rhythm.

Nelly had a unique approach to hip-hop that made him hard to classify. He'd grown up halfway between the Midwest and the South, so his voice had both a country twang and a Southern drawl. When he rapped, he also sang, which gave his music a catchy, sing-along style that was missing from a lot of hip-hop music. Not everyone liked it—but plenty of people did.

When the single from the album was released in February 2000, it rose to number one on *Billboard*'s rap singles chart and it stayed there for four weeks. Then it jumped across the gap between rap and pop music, and pop radio stations began playing the song as well. Nelly told *Jet* magazine, "I don't sound like anyone . . . I'm rappin' the blues."

Women listeners were particularly taken with Nelly. "I've got a lot of female fans," Nelly told *Rolling Stone*. "Well, don't get mad at me because I appeal more to women. I can't help it. I'm sorry. It would have been better if I was ugly."

But it wasn't just women who were buying Nelly's CD. By the end of August 2000, the album had reached number one on *Billboard*, and there it stayed for a total of six weeks. Eventually, it went on to sell more than eight million copies.

Another single from the album, "E.I.," hit *Billboard*'s top ten in December. The year ended with Nelly as the Top Hot Rap Artist—Male for *Billboard*'s year-end chart. The year 2000 had been an incredible one for Nelly.

This was the year when everything turned around for him. From drug dealing on the streets of St. Louis, he had made the incredible leap to success, fame, and fortune. The year 2001 would be even better.

Riding the Wave

"You have a lifetime to do your first album," Nelly said backstage at the Billboard Music Awards in 2001, "and eighteen months for your second." Nelly knew that his second CD would prove whether he really had what it takes.

"It's just a matter of drawing on the talent I have inside," he said. But would his talent be enough?

While he was working on his next album, Nelly was getting plenty of **affirmation** that he did indeed have what it took to make it in

In 2001, Nelly performed with Justin Timberlake at the *Billboard* Awards. *Country Grammar* turned multiplatinum and there seemed to be no stopping Nelly. Cornell Haynes Jr. had come a long way from the poor, angry little boy in St. Louis, Missouri.

the hip-hop world. Not only did *Country Grammar* sell well; it also earned him award after award. Each honor reinforced Nelly's belief in his talent, and each award added to his fame and popularity. Nelly was riding a huge wave of success and achievement that showed no sign of crashing.

By the end of 2001, Nelly had won Artist of the Year at the Billboard Awards; Favorite Hip-Hop Artist at the American Music Awards; the BET Award for Best New Artist; the MTV Video Music Award for the Best Rap Video (for the single "Ride Wit Me"); the Blockbuster

True to its word, Nelly's record company released an album by the St. Lunatics, and Nelly did his part to promote it. Here, in this 2001 photo, Nelly is shown signing autographs to promote the band's album, *Free City*.

Entertainment Award for Favorite Male—New Artist; two Source awards for Album of the Year and New Artist of the Year; and the Soul Train Award for the Best New Artist. *People* magazine named him as one of its "Breakthrough Stars." Although he did not win a Grammy Award, he was nominated for two (Best Rap Album and Best Rap Solo Performance).

Nelly was making a name for himself, and people across America were paying attention. When he performed "Walk This Way" with Aerosmith and 'NSync at the 2001 Super Bowl halftime show, millions of people got to know who Nelly was. When he played with the group Jagged Edge on "Where the Party At" from their album *Jagged Little Thrill*, he made it to *Billboard*'s top-ten list yet again. His song "#1," the first song on the soundtrack for the movie *Training Day* starring Denzel Washington, was the icing on the cake. It too hit the top forty on *Billboard*.

In 2001, the St. Lunatics got their chance as well. Their CD, *Free City*, didn't turn out to be the bestseller that *Country Grammar* was. But it did show that the group could stick together. Their loyalty to each other meant something to them all.

Nelly had come a long way—and he hadn't stopped yet.

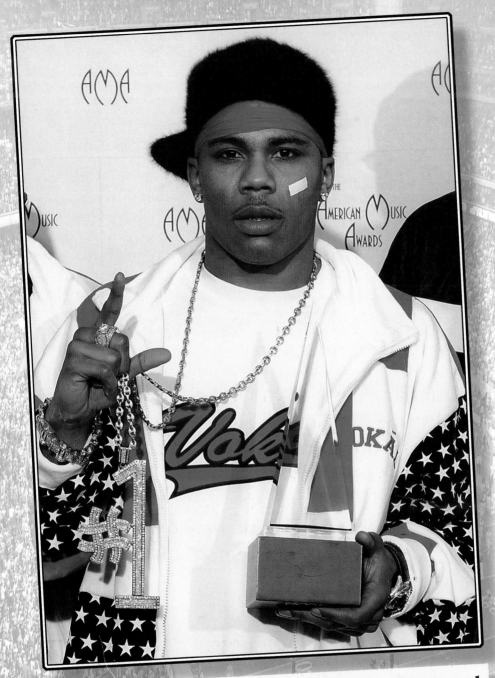

Nelly's popularity soared with the release of his second album, *Nellyville*. The album stayed in the top spot on the charts for three weeks. It also brought him many awards. In this photo, Nelly shows off his American Music Award for Favorite Rap/Hip Hop artist.

3

Going All the Way

January 2002 found Nelly with his hometown Rams at the Super Bowl—and Nelly performing during the halftime show. He told *People* magazine, "It was the highlight of my life." The Rams may have lost to the New England Patriots, but that disappointment didn't cloud Nelly's excitement. The year 2002 was off to a great start.

Nellyville

Nelly's second album was this year's focus. Its title song, "Nellyville," described an imaginary place where Nelly was the mayor and all the inhabitants had forty acres of land and a pool.

When the CD was released on June 25, it entered the *Billboard* charts at number one. First-week sales totaled at more than 714,000 units, and it stayed at number one for three weeks. After only a month, it was triple **platinum**.

The CD's sales were boosted by the summer's hot single from the album, "Hot in Herre." The song was on *Billboard*'s Hot 100 for seven weeks. "Hot in Herre" was followed by another single from *Nellyville*, "Dilemma." Kelly Rowland from the group Destiny's Child had added her voice to the song, which turned out to be the first rap song to stay at number one on the *Billboard* list for ten consecutive weeks. Nelly ended up tied with Elton John as the male solo artist with the most consecutive weeks at number one on *Billboard*'s Hot 100.

In September of 2002, Nelly went on tour, allowing his fans to see him in person. They loved him. With his hand held high in an L-shape (for Lunatics), Nelly was riding high. But the tour was marred with violence when a concert-goer was stabbed to death after Nelly's concert in San Diego, California.

Despite this tragedy, in many ways, 2002 was even more exciting than the year before had been for Nelly. His music rode the top of the charts across the Atlantic in the United Kingdom, while back home in the United States, the television show *Saturday Night Live* asked him to perform. *Nellyville* was certified as five-times platinum. It ended 2002 as the year's second-biggest-selling album.

What's more, the album brought more awards Nelly's way. He won the 2002 American Music Award for Favorite Rap/Hip-Hop Artist, and he won six *Billboard* awards, including Artist of the Year (and was nominated for eight other categories as well). *Teen People* featured him as one of its 25 Hottest Stars Under 25. *Entertainment Weekly* ranked him at number thirty-nine on its 101 Most Powerful list. Teen Choice awarded him Choice Single and Choice Hook Up awards for his single "Girlfriend" (performed with 'NSync), as well as Choice Song of the Summer for "Hot in Herre." The video for "#1" was nominated for two MTV awards, and so was his **collaboration** with 'NSync.

But he still didn't have his Grammy. He was nominated for two Grammys in 2002 but didn't win any awards.

2003

At the 2003 Grammys, however, all that changed. This time, Nelly was nominated for six awards—and he brought home two: one for Male Rap Solo Performance and another for his collaboration with Destiny Child's Kelly Rowland. He also performed at the Grammy awards ceremony.

The next month, Nelly won the Soul Train Music Award for Best R&B Soul or Rap Album of the Year. He was also honored with the Sammy Davis Jr. Award for Entertainer of the Year.

And the year kept getting better. In April, Nickelodeon gave him the Kids' Choice Award for Favorite Male Singer. By June, *Nellyville* was certified as six-times platinum. By the end of the summer, his single "Shake Ya Tailfeather" (which included performances by P. Diddy and

Despite his album's success and the many awards it received, Nelly was disappointed at the 44th Annual Grammy Awards when he went home with none. Still, his performance at the ceremony had an enthusiastic audience.

Nelly's Grammy drought ended at the 45th Annual Grammy Awards in 2003. Nominated for multiple Grammys, Nelly won two awards, including Best Rap/Sung Collaboration with Kelly Rowland of Destiny's Child. The crowd was treated to an airborne Nelly during his performance at the ceremony.

Murphy Lee) had hit *Billboard*'s top-ten list, and it stayed there for week after week. In October, the song won a Radio Music Award for Best Driving Song. The same month, Nelly took home a Source Award for Artist of the Year. Meanwhile, another single, "Iz U," was climbing the top-forty lists as well.

In November of 2003, Nelly released a **remix** album titled *La Derrty Versions*. By December, it had already gone platinum.

2004

In 2004, Nelly won another Grammy, one he shared with P. Diddy and Murphy Lee. "Shake Ya Tailfeather" earned Best Rap Performance by a Duo or Group.

Nelly's creative juices kept on flowing. Later that year, he released two albums on the same day: *Sweat* and *Suit*. He told *Jet*, "Guns N Roses and Bruce Springsteen did it, but I'm the first hip-hop performer and the first African American to do that." Nelly didn't release the two albums simultaneously because he wanted to break any records, though. "I didn't know that at the time," he continued to *Jet*. "I just wanted to do it because it was a way for me to get a lot of music out and get a chance to do both sides." The music on *Sweat* is aimed at clubs— it's music for dancing—while *Suit* has more mellow rap love songs. The St. Lunatics were featured on *Sweat*, and rap star Mase came out of retirement to be part of *Suit*.

Sometimes Nelly has been criticized for his willingness to mix hip-hop with any style of music. But Nelly knows that his mixtures work for his fans. On *Suit*, he joined up with country music great Tim McGraw for the song "Over and Over." Nelly told *Newsweek*, "[Tim's] a guy's guy. You know, I get along with guy guys. If you like sports, music and cars and all that, then you and I will get along just fine." When Nelly spoke with VH1, he added:

> **"Me and Tim just clicked for some reason. I got the chance to hoop with Tim at the charity events and that was hot. Here it is, I have this white boy out here and he is hoopin' for real. He was shootin' nice. Then we had the chance to talk and holla, and he was cool. We had similar backgrounds, being . . . not so much on our own, but growing up with similar problems and issues."**

On September 14, 2004, Nelly became the first hip-hop artist to release two albums on the same day. *Sweat* featured dance music aimed at the club crowd. The St. Lunatics were featured on that album.

Hip-hop **purists** may have gotten their feathers ruffled by Nelly's willingness to cross the lines, but his fans liked the sound. The song topped both the *Billboard* chart and the Rhythmic Airplay list. In November 2004, it hit number one on the charts, and it stayed there for another four weeks. By the end of the year, *Sweat* had gone platinum, and *Suit* was certified two-times platinum.

Suit was the other album released on September 14, 2004. Songs on this album were more mellow. Retired rap star Mase performed on Suit. In 2005, Nelly released Sweatsuit, which included songs from both Sweat and Suit.

The Sky's the Limit

In 2005, Nelly was the first hip-hop artist to be nominated for a Country Music Award for his collaboration with Tim McGraw on "Over and Over." In February, Nelly was nominated for another Grammy. Although he didn't go home with a trophy, he was still going strong.

Who would have thought to combine the talents of Nelly and country music star Tim McGraw? Well, someone did, and, in 2005, Nelly became the first hip-hop artist to be nominated for a Country Music Award for his number-one duet with McGraw.

Another of his singles, "N Dey Say," made the top forty, while the singles "Hot in Herre," "Tilt Ya Head Back," and "My Place" went **gold**; "Get It Poppin'" was certified platinum, and "Over and Over" went platinum two times. *Suit* was certified three-times platinum.

To keep things moving, Nelly released *Sweatsuit*, which included highlights from the two previous albums, as well as a few new tunes. His voice was heard on the Notorious B.I.G. **posthumous** collection, *Duets: The Final Chapter*. And last but certainly not least, Nelly released a single from *Sweatsuit*, a song he'd done with Paul Wall called "Grillz."

"Grillz" showcases the street trend of putting removable jewelry on the teeth. The song was promoted as a "street" single, not intended for big publicity, but it took everyone by surprise. By January 2006, it was topping *Billboard*'s charts, staying at number one on the rap chart for five weeks in a row, while at the same time it was number one on the R&B/Hip-Hop charts for three weeks in a row. By the end of the month, the song's video was number one on MTV and BET.

After only a few years, Nelly's career had shot sky high. But music wasn't the only item on Nelly's plate. He had a few others there as well.

While still struggling with the St. Lunatics in St. Louis, Nelly had launched his own clothing line, *Vokal*. In 2001, it went public, just one of Nelly's non-music ventures. This photo is from a 2002 photo shoot promoting Vokal.

4

Outside the Music World

Nelly's proved he has what it takes to be successful in the music world—but he's also worked hard in others areas of life, including business and charities. After a childhood of poverty, Nelly seems determined to rise as high as he can in the world, as fast as he can. Along the way, he hasn't forgotten to help others.

Vokal Clothing

Nellie started his own clothing line, Vokal, back in 1997, before his musical career had begun. It was a pretty low-budget operation at first: he and his partners sold hats and T-shirts from their apartments and out of the back of a car. But the company grew. Just like Nelly's music career, Vokal went national in 2001.

The company's product line consisted mostly of athletic wear, and included velour and fleece loungewear as well. Vokal representatives toured with the St. Lunatics, hustling T-shirts and jerseys after their concerts. As Nelly's music career grew, so did Vokal. In 2003, Vokal introduced a woman's line—Apple Bottoms. And Nelly was searching for new ways to promote his company.

The Sports World

In 2003, Nelly bought into the Craftsman Truck team, which participated in NASCAR (National Association for Stock Car Racing). His connection with NASCAR gave his clothing line more visibility—and brought Nelly new fans from around the country.

Nelly has pursued his love of sports in another way as well. He's part owner of a professional basketball team, the Charlotte Bobcats.

Nelly the Entrepreneur

Nelly has proved that he knows how to market not only music and clothing, but most everything else as well. By 2005, Nelly had turned into an **entrepreneur**. Nelly is the CEO (chief executive officer) of his very own company, Derrty Entertainment. The company includes Vokal and Apple Bottoms, as well as a record label. It even produces an energy juice called Pimp Juice.

During the first three months Pimp Juice was on the market, it sold over a million units. The Beverage Network, a respected beverage industry trade organization, recognized the drink as People's Choice for best energy drink, and *Vibe* magazine agreed.

In January 2006, Nelly's business bought into a new venture—a bar and grill in Hazelwood, Missouri. He named it Mack's Bar and Grill, which contains the first letters of its owners: Murphy Lee, Ali, Slo Down, Kyjuan, and Cornell. The restaurant has flat-screen TVs for music videos and sports programs, and it serves hamburgers and fries.

According to the St. Louis *Post-Dispatch*, the city welcomed Nelly's restaurant. "We wish them the best," said Hazelwood mayor T. R. Carr. "Everything they presented to the council looks pretty positive." A local lawyer, Herman Jimerson, agreed: "I believe it is good to spend back in the community. I am glad that [Nelly] as a young artist is doing this."

Nelly's Acting Career

In 2002, Nelly made his **debut** acting appearance. He had the starring role in the independently released film *Snipes*. Three years later, fans had a chance to see Nelly in the remake of *The Longest Yard*, where he played a jailbird football player named Earl. (He also produced and appeared on the movie's soundtrack.)

Nelly enjoyed the chance to take on the role of a sports player. After all, had things turned out differently, his life might have been very like Earl's. "It wasn't a stretch at all," he told VH1. "I can play running back. And it's not like I haven't been in jail before."

Nelly also stars in the 2007 film *Crenshaw Boulevard*. And he hopes to have the chance to show his acting talent on the little screen as well. A. Smith and Co., the production company behind a number of TV reality shows, plans to have camera crews tail Nelly, keeping track of his day-to-day life. "I look forward to showing my fans what my world is

In 2005, fans all over the world were able to catch Nelly's acting skills when he appeared as a football player in the remake of *The Longest Yard*, with Adam Sandler and Chris Rock. Nelly also produced the movie's soundtrack.

about and bringing more attention to my nonprofit organizations," Nelly said in a press release.

Charity

Nelly's nonprofit work is high on his priorities. While he was busy making money in the music and clothing industry, he never forgot the kids who were still back in the hood where he had grown up. He started a charity called 4Sho4Kids, which provided disadvantaged youngsters in St. Louis with medical treatment and **literacy** programs. The agency focuses particularly on kids who were born addicted to drugs or who have **Down syndrome**.

Missouri governor Bob Holden honored Nelly and the rest of the St. Lunatics for the good work they had done. "They're to be applauded for giving back to a community that has embraced them," he said to reporter Steven Chean.

Nelly recognizes his good fortune, and he credits his friends from the St. Lunatics for helping him to rise above his circumstances. He told Chean:

> **"Workin' with the 'Tics saved me when people on my block were either locked up or dead. It can be turned around, and that's what I try to tell kids living the same way I was."**

When Nelly spoke with *Twist* magazine, he added, "You have to give back. It's a must-do thing."

Nelly uses his other business ventures to help support his charity work. For example, a portion of all proceeds from Pimp Juice goes to 4Sho4Kids. Nelly created the Positive. Intellectual. Motivated. Person. (P.I.M.P.) Scholars Program, a scholarship that's designed to aid students who not only work hard at academics, but who also are leaders in extracurricular activities.

One part of the work that 4Sho4Kids Foundation does is called R.A.P.—which stand for Real Academic Progress. R.A.P.'s goal is to help kids prepare themselves for a "life of learning through a focus on Reading, Math, Language Arts, and Test taking skills." According to R.A.P.'s mission statement, the organization is "committed to the self-worth of each individual and embraces the belief that 'NO CHILD WILL BE LEFT OUT.'" On its Web site, R.A.P. lists for children these steps for success:

Kids are important to Nelly. All his business projects support his charity 4Sho4Kids Foundation, which provides medical treatments and literacy programs for disadvantaged children in the St. Louis area. Here, Nelly and his aunt are shown at a 2005 auction to benefit the foundation.

"Be On Time
Be a Goal Setter
Be a Hard Worker
Be Friendly
Be a Good Listener
Be a Risk Taker"

Nelly even uses food to raise money for good causes. In 2003, he contributed a dish to a fund-raiser for the St. Louis Zoo. Here, he and band member Slo Down are shown with one of Nelly's favorite foods, mini potatoes with blue cheese.

Aside from the work of his own foundations, Nelly takes part in many charity events as well. After the terrorist attacks of September 11, 2001, Nelly used his birthday party as an occasion to raise funds for the victims' families. In 2003, he helped out the St. Louis Zoo, contributing a dish for a celebrity fundraising dinner. The following year, Nelly got involved with P. Diddy's efforts to encourage young African Americans to get out and vote.

By 2005, Nelly had signed on to warn the American public of the dangers of underage drinking. In a press release, he said:

> **"Underage drinking is a very serious issue, and working with parents to address the problem is the responsible thing to do. It's very important for parents to talk with their children about everything, and underage drinking is definitely one of those things you need to jump on early."**

Anheuser-Busch sponsored a thirty-second TV ad, where Nelly pretended to be a chef, a boxer, and a golfer, all in an effort to get his message across.

After Hurricane Katrina hit America's Gulf Coast, Nelly was one of the many musicians who did what he could to raise funds for those who had lost their homes. He took part in the Fashion Rocks event at Radio City Music Hall in New York City, where all proceeds were donated to Hurricane Katrina relief work.

Nelly works hard to help those who are in need. Although some people have criticized him for his preoccupation with money, Nelly insists that people don't really know the "real" Nelly if they judge him only by his public image. Family, friends, and foes all have very different perspectives on who Nelly Haynes really is.

When Nelly's sister Jackie was diagnosed with cancer, he used his star power to help her find a bone marrow donor. Though their efforts were unsuccessful, the Jes Us 4 Jackie Foundation increased awareness in the black community of the need for bone marrow donations.

5

Family, Fans, and Foes

People are shaped by others. Nelly's family, his fans, even his enemies, all influenced him. In the end, though, the decision was up to him. He could have chosen to stay on the streets, selling drugs. The choices he made instead were not always popular; they may not have always been right; but Nelly had come a long way from the hood.

Family

Families can be sources of strength, but they can also cause pain. Nelly's parents failed to provide him with the security he craved as a child. Despite this, he looked up to his mother while he was growing up, but his relationship with his father was stormy. According to the IMDb Web site, he said, "I probably cried only five or six times in my life and I think four of those times was from my daddy kicking my butt."

Nelly's relationship with the St. Lunatics gave him the steadiness he had craved; they were like another, more dependable family. But one of the hard times in Nelly's life came in 2001, when he lost a member of his crew. His half-brother, City Spud, was sentenced to ten years in prison for robbery. "We're not sure when he's getting out," Nelly told *Rolling Stone*. "We're working on that." While his brother was in prison, Nelly wore a Band-Aid on his left cheek, as a constant reminder of City Spud.

There were more hard times to come. In 2005, Nelly's older sister Jackie Donohue lost a three-year battle with **leukemia** when she was only thirty-one years old. Nelly had done all that he could to help his sister. When she needed a bone marrow transplant and couldn't find a donor match, he helped her begin the Jes Us 4 Jackie campaign to raise public awareness of the need for more bone marrow and **stem cell** donations. (Out of the 5.3 million donors registered with the National Marrow Donor Program in 2004, only 423,000 were African American; since the best matches usually come from people with similar racial backgrounds, this means that blacks who need bone marrow or stem cell transplants may not be able to find a match.) Together, the brother and sister had worked to enroll more donors, especially among African Americans and other minorities. But they never found a match for Jackie.

Nelly does his best to keep his private feelings just that—private. He made public statements about Jackie, because he felt it was important that he speak out on behalf of bone marrow donations. But when it comes to his children, Nelly protects their privacy fiercely. He has never revealed who their mother is, and even the dates of their births are uncertain. Being a parent is clearly important to Nelly, though. On his *Suit* album, in the song "Die for You," he reveals just how much he cares about his children. He takes being a father seriously—but he also enjoys the fun times. "I've done the Funky Chicken and the Hokey Pokey," Nelly told *J-14* magazine. "I have two kids. I've done the Macarena with my kids."

Fans

Audiences love Nelly. Crowds go wild when he shouts his trademark chants, "E.I., E.I.!" (which means, "Yes! Bring it on!") and "Uh-oh, uh-oh!" His fans follow his example, wearing sports jerseys backward and taping Band-Aids on their cheeks.

Nelly loves the attention, and he understands that people notice whatever he does. However, he wants his fans to understand that they should look to people who are closer to them for their role models. He told VH1:

"I always like to say, I don't see athletes and entertainers as role models, because you don't know the whole role of my life. You can be inspirations for people who are in a bad situation, but I think a role model should be someone who is closest to you. You should be able to see their whole role in life, how they carry themselves every day, and not just when they are on TV or in magazines. You don't know everything I have been through and how I dealt with it. . . . I say, be *better* than Nelly. Be better than me."

The fans love Nelly, and Nelly loves the fans. His fans even adopted his trademarks—wearing a Band-Aid on their cheek and their sports jerseys backward. Here, Nelly signs autographs at a 2001 charity basketball game in suburban St. Louis, Missouri.

GET YOUR VOTE ON! THE ULTIMATE ELECTION GUIDE

VIBE

www.vibe.com

WHAT'S THE WORD ON
NELLY

Pop star, pimp,
or gangsta?

The last
days of
RICK
JAMES

NBA
REPORT
The good
ball young

U.S. $3.99/CAN $5.50 NOVEMBER 2004

PLUS
FANTASIA
TALIB KWELI
SLIM THUG
JADAKISS

Not everybody loves Nelly. Critics and fellow artists have often criticized him for selling out to pop music by performing with non–hip-hop singers. The controversy surrounding Nelly was the cover story in the November 2004 issue of *Vibe*.

Foes

Nelly's fans love him—but the music critics don't always agree. Fellow hip-hop artists have also criticized Nelly's approach to rap. They accuse him of selling out to pop music. They point to his collaboration on his second album with boy-band star Justin Timberlake as proof that Nelly doesn't stay true to hip-hop's roots.

Nelly objected. He told the *New York Times*:

"Justin is a fan of hip-hop. It's all hip-hop, but you got people trying to divide it saying what it is and what it's not. You going to walk around a roomful of kids and tell them they wrong?"

Feminists aren't too fond of Nelly, either. They criticize him for the way he portrays women in his songs and videos. In February 2004, students in the Feminist Majority Leadership Alliance at Spelman College (a historically black women's college) voted Nelly **Misogynist** of the Month. The Spelman chapter of the NAACP (National Association for the Advancement of Colored People) got involved as well, and a protest was planned that made Nelly cancel a bone-marrow drive he had planned for the campus on behalf of Jes Us 4 Jackie. The uproar gained national media attention.

Students claimed they had singled out Nelly because they were disgusted by the video for his song "Tip Drill." (A "tip drill" is urban slang for a woman with an attractive body and an ugly face.) The video was too explicit for regular television, but it aired on BET's *Uncut*, a late-night program that features racy hip-hop videos. Nelly's video portrayed half-naked women accepting a credit card as payment for sexual favors.

Nelly was furious that the protests had made his foundation cancel its bone-marrow drive. "You are talking about a video, as opposed to saving a life," he told CNN. "If you took half the time you took to really discuss my video and my problems to discuss what we're really trying to do, then you can educate so many more people."

In response to Nelly's criticism, the students held their own bone-marrow drive at Atlanta's West End mall and registered three hundred donors. "I couldn't handle the thought that someone would not get a transplant because our drive had been cancelled," Asha Jennings, the president of Spelman's student government, told the *Chronicle of Higher Education*. She added:

> **"I'm just trying to speak for all the children who don't have the same level of education as me. They don't know what it is to say no to these images. . . . People weren't really discussing this a few months ago, and just the fact that they are now means that we had a positive impact."**

Nelly tried to defend himself to *Newsweek*:

> **"I mean, we're not *forcing* the women to do it. The [women] come in, they read, they know exactly what is called for. They all have to be of age, and this is what they choose to do. Considering that 85 percent of my fans [are] women, I don't think women would support me the way they do if they thought that I was actually demeaning to them. I don't think that if they thought my purpose was to ridicule, that they would put up with me, and support my music. I give women more credit than that."**

Other people criticize Nelly because he ignores hip-hop's political power. He told *Blender* magazine, "Some people don't want politics in their music. Some people want their music . . . so they can have fun and dance." But hip-hop music has always been a powerful force; the classic rappers used hip-hop to shout their anger against an unfair world, and more and more of today's big-name rappers—including Russell Simmons, Jay-Z, and P. Diddy—are speaking out on political issues.

Aaron Bernard, a hip-hop **activist**, is disappointed by Nelly's statements to *Blender*. He said to BlackAmericaweb.com:

> **"That's basically a slap in the face to . . . others who have come before him and changed the face of hip-hop more than he ever will. . . . It's sad for somebody in his generation of hip-hop to say something like that because he sells so many records and has so much influence."**

Critics like Bernard say that Nelly's take on hip-hop represents the wide gap that lies between the true hip-hop culture and the mainstream

While some have criticized Nelly for ignoring the politics of hip-hop, few argue with his charity work. In 2005, HSAN recognized Nelly and Michelle Williams of Destiny's Child for their charitable contributions. Shown here are (left to right): Russell Simmons, Williams, Nelly, and Benjamin Chavez.

appeal of rap music that is driven by sales only. "For him to say keep politics out of the music is basically saying he's not hip-hop," Greg Thomas, a professor at Syracuse University, told BlackAmericaweb.com. "How do you have black music without politics?"

Of course, while some people are criticizing Nelly and his music, plenty of other people are simply buying his music and enjoying it. Still, other critics aren't happy with the language Nelly uses in his songs and in his interviews. They don't like that he called his energy drink Pimp Juice, and they're not happy that his program that gives college grants to students is called P.I.M.P. These are jokes for Nelly—but not everyone gets the humor.

Though fans might think they know the "real" Nelly, he has worked hard to keep parts of his life private. The world will just have to be content with his music and his charity work.

The Real Nelly

Nelly's critics may think they know who he is, and so may his fans. But ultimately, Nelly is a private person who doesn't always show his deepest nature. He uses humor as a way to hide himself—but in the end, actions speak louder than words.

The boy who grew up in St. Louis and loved sports hasn't changed all that much. Nelly told *Newsweek*:

> **"I love sports. . . . I thought baseball would be my way. A *lot* of people thought that baseball would be the way for me. But, unfortunately, we make some decisions in our lifetime that deter us from sticking to the plan. I think the alternative turned out pretty well."**

The little boy in St. Louis was often angry with the world—but he turned away from violence and allowed his anger to drive him to success. "I'm a competitor," he told *Newsweek*. "I've spent my whole life listening to people tell me I can't, I won't and I'm not. You say I can't, I will."

1940s The blues combines with jazz and R&B is born.

1970s Cornell Haynes Jr. (Nelly) is born on November 2 in Austin, Texas.

1997 Starts clothing line called Vokal, which goes national in 2001.

2000 Releases his first album, *Country Grammar*.

Is named Top Hot Male Rap Artist by *Billboard*.

August *Country Grammar* is number one on *Billboard* charts.

2001 Nelly performs at the Super Bowl halftime show.

St. Lunatics release their first album.

Wins *Billboard* award, American Music Award, BET Award, MTV Music Award, Blockbuster Entertainment Award, Source awards, and Soul Train Award.

2002 "Dilemma" becomes the first rap single to stay at number one on *Billboard* for ten consecutive weeks.

Nellyville becomes the second-biggest-selling album of the year.

Nelly makes his film debut in *Snipes*.

Wins American Music Awards, six *Billboard* awards, named one of *Teen People*'s 25 Hottest Stars Under 25, named to *Entertainment Weekly*'s 101 Most Powerful list, won Teen Choice awards, and two MTV awards.

Performs at the Super Bowl halftime show.

Releases his record-breaking second album, *Nellyville*.

Goes on tour.

2003 Buys a share in a NASCAR truck team.

Introduces Pimp Juice, an energy drink.

Starts the Jes Us 4 Jackie campaign to search for a bone marrow donor for his sister Jackie.

Wins two Grammys, two Soul Train Music awards, a Radio Music Award, and a Source Award.

Releases a remix album *La Derrty Versions*.

2004 Wins Grammy for "Shake Ya Tailfeather."

The Feminist Majority Leadership Alliance names Nelly Misogynist of the Month,

Releases two albums simultaneously, one rap and one R&B.

2005 Becomes the first hip-hop artist to be nominated for a Country Music Award.

Becomes part owner of the NBA Charlotte Bobcats.

Participates in Fashion Rocks to raise funds for Hurricane Katrina relief efforts.

Teams with Anheuser-Busch to combat underage drinking.

Sister Jackie dies of leukemia.

2006 Opens Mack's Bar and Grill in Hazelwood, Missouri.

Discography
Solo Albums

2000   *Country Grammar*

2002   *Hot in Here*
         Nellyville

2003   *Da Derrty Versions: The Reinvention*

2004   *Sweat Suit Combo*
         Sweat
         Suit

Number-one Singles

2000   "(Hot S**t) Country Grammar"

2002   "Hot in Herre"
         "Dilemma"

2003   "Shake Ya Tailfeather"
         "Air Force Ones"

2005   "Grillz"

Selected Television Appearances

2000   *Jenny Jones*

2001   *Mad TV*; *Snipes*; *The 25 Hottest Stars Under 25*; *Cribs*

2002   *Saturday Night Live*

2003   *Hip Hop Babylon*; *Mad TV*; *Cedric the Entertainer Presents*;
         Tinseltown TV; *The Tonight Show with Jay Leno*

2004   *Big Time*; *The Dome*; *Mad TV*; *The Maury Povich Show*;
         Saturday Night Live; *The Tonight Show with Jay Leno*;
         Top of the Pops Saturday; *The Late Late Show with Craig
         Kilborn*; *Last Call with Carson Daly*; *The View*; *Jimmy
         Kimmel Live*; *TV Total*

2005   *The Sharon Osbourne Show*; *An All-Star Salute to Patti LaBelle:
         Live from Atlantis*; *Tsunami Aid: A Concert of Hope*; *Beef 3*;
         Ellen: The Ellen DeGeneres Show*; *Inked*; *The View*; *The
         Tonight Show with Jay Leno*; *Jimmy Kimmel Live*

2006   *Ellen: The Ellen DeGeneres Show*

Film

2005   *The Longest Yard*
2006   *Crenshaw Blvd.*

Video

2003   *Justin Timberlake: Justified—The Videos*

Awards

2001   BET Awards: Best New Artist

Blockbuster Entertainer Awards: Favorite New Male Artist

MTV Video Music Awards: Best Rap Video

Proclamation from the State of Missouri by Governor Holden for his work as an advocate of education

Soul Train Awards: Best R&B/Soul or Rap New Artist

Source Awards: Best New Artist; Album of the Year

World Music Award: Best New Artist

2002   American Music Awards: Favorite Rap/Hip-Hop Artist

Billboard Music Awards: Artist of the Year; Male Artist of the Year; Male Hot 100 Artist of the Year; Male R&B/Hip-Hop Artist of the Year; Rap Artist of the Year; Rap Track of the Year ("Hot in Herre")

2003   Grammy Awards: Best Rap/Sung Collaboration (with Kelly Rowland); Best Male Rap Solo Performance

Kid's Choice Award: Favorite Male Singer

MTV Awards: Best R&B Video; Best Hip-Hop Video

Soul Train Awards: Sammy Davis Jr. Entertainer of the Year

Source Awards: Source Foundation Image Award; Artist of the Year—Male

Grammy Awards: Best Rap Performance by a Duo or Group (with Murphy Lee and P. Diddy)

Books

Bankston, John. *Nelly*. Hockessin, Del.: Mitchell Lane, 2004.

Kenyatta, Kelly. *So You Want to Be a Hip Hop Star—Your Complete Guide: Featuring Nelly, Eminem, Eve, 50 Cent, & Other Great Rappers.* Chicago: William H. Kelly, 2006.

Malone, Bonz, Nichole Beattie, and Di Lindy. *Hip-Hop Immortals: The Remix.* New York: Thunder's Mouth Press, 2003.

Nelly. *Nelly—Selections from Sweat/Suit.* Milwaukee, Wis.: Hal Leonard, 2005.

Magazines

Bozza, Anthony. "Nelly." *Rolling Stone*, November 9, 2000.

Christian, Margena A. "The Two Sides of Nelly." *Jet*, September 13, 2004.

Habib, Daniel G. "Q&A: Nelly." *Sports Illustrated*, August 19, 2002.

Hall, Rashaun. "Nelly's World Heated Up in 2002." *Billboard*, December 7, 2002.

People Magazine. "Nelly." December 31, 2002.

Sanneh, Kalefa. "The Mayor of Nellyville." *New York Times*, June 23, 2002, p. 21.

Wasfie, Giselle. "Go Nellie." *Teen People*, August 20, 2002, p. 120.

Web Sites

4Sho4Kids Foundation
www.4sho4kids.org

Jes Us 4 Jackie
www.jesus4jackie.com

Nelly
www.mtv.com/music/#/music/artist/nelly/artist.jhtml

Nelly
www.rollingstone.com/artists/nelly

Official Nelly Web Site
www.nelly.net

activist—someone who vigorously and sometimes aggressively pursues a political or social goal.

affirmation—positive statement of achievement or indication of worth.

collaboration—the act of working together.

currency—money.

debut—to show or perform something for the first time.

demo—a recorded sample of music.

Down syndrome—a congenital condition characterized by mental retardation, slanted eyes, and broad hands with short fingers.

emceeing—acting as master of ceremonies for an event.

entrepreneur—someone who assumes the risks and benefits of operating a business.

feminists—people who believe in the need to secure rights and opportunities for women that are equal to those available for men.

gold—signifies the sale of more than 500,000 CDs.

gospel—highly emotional evangelical vocal music that originated among African Americans in the South.

heritage—a country's, area's, or individual's history.

hood—slang for a neighborhood.

inequity—a lack of fairness or justice.

leukemia—a type of cancer in which white blood cells displace normal blood.

literacy—the ability to read and write on a competent level.

misogynist—someone who hates women as a group.

platinum—signifies the sale of more than 2 million CDs.

posthumous—occurring after death.

prejudice—a usually unfavorable opinion based on insufficient knowledge, irrational feelings, or inaccurate stereotypes.

purists—those who insist on maintaining something in its original, traditional form.

recruited—enrolled someone as a worker or member.

remix—a new version of a piece of music.

scouts—someone sent to evaluate athletes for possible recruitment.

segregation—forced separation of racial groups.

spirituals—folk hymns.

stem cell—an undifferentiated cell from which specialized cells can develop.

studio musicians—musicians employed by a music production company to perform backup on recordings.

James Hooper grew up to the sound of drumbeats. His brother, a drummer, rapped and tapped on any surface he could find, and James gained a love of rhythm. Although James pursued a career in writing rather than music, he has never lost his appreciation for his brother's world. James has written previously for newspapers and magazines, and welcomes any chance to describe the world of music with words.

Picture Credits

page

2: AFP/Lucy Nicholson
8: UPI/Bill Greenblatt
11: Zuma Press/Courtesy Haynes Family
12: Zuma Press/Courtesy Haynes Family
14: Tina Paul/WENN
17: Zuma Press/Courtesy Haynes Family
18: Zuma Press/Steven Tackeff
20: KRT/NMI
23: Zuma Press/Steven Tackeff
25: Reuters/Ethan Miller
26: UPI/Bill Greenblatt
28: AFP/Lucy Nicholson

31: AFP/Hector Mata
32: Reuters/Fred Prouser
34: PRNewsFoto/NMI
35: PRNewsFoto/NMI
36: SHNS/Justin Lubin/NBC Universal
38: Zuma Press/Mario Ruiz
41: Paramount Pictures/NMI
43: PNP/WENN
44: UPI/Bill Greenblatt
46: UPI/Bill Greenblatt
49: UPI/Bill Greenblatt
50: WENN Photos
53: Zuma Press/Aviv Small
54: KRT/NMI

Front cover: PRNewsFoto/NMI
Back cover: G. Ohlenbostel/Action Press